Camila Batmanghelidjh
and Kids Company
Mind the Child
**The Victoria Line**

Danny Dorling
The 32 Stops
**The Central Line**

Fantastic Man
Buttoned-Up
**The East London Line**

John Lanchester
What We Talk About When
We Talk About The Tube
**The District Line**

William Leith
A Northern Line Minute
**The Northern Line**

Richard Mabey
A Good Parcel of
English Soil
**The Metropolitan Line**

Paul Morley
Earthbound
**The Bakerloo Line**

John O'Farrell
A History of Capitalism
According to the
Jubilee Line
**The Jubilee Line**

Philippe Parreno
Drift
**The Hammersmith & City Line**

Leanne Shapton
Waterloo–City,
City–Waterloo
**The ...one – & City Line** ...068.

Lucy Wadham
In gov.uk/libraries

Peter York

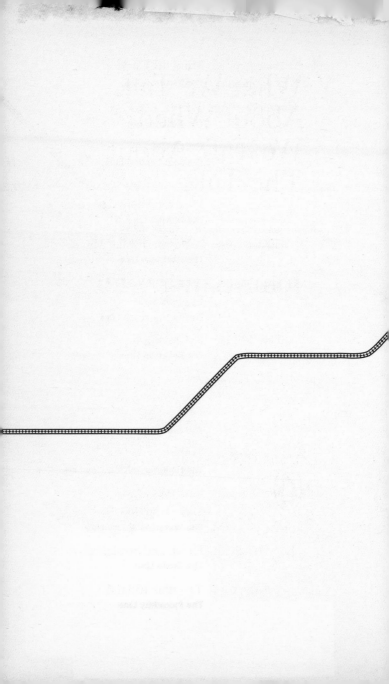

# What We Talk About When We Talk About The Tube

## John Lanchester

PENGUIN BOOKS

PENGUIN BOOKS

Published by the Penguin Group
Penguin Books Ltd, 80 Strand, London WC2R 0RL, England
Penguin Group (USA) Inc., 375 Hudson Street, New York, New York 10014, USA
Penguin Group (Canada), 90 Eglinton Avenue East, Suite 700, Toronto, Ontario,
Canada M4P 2Y3 (a division of Pearson Penguin Canada Inc.)
Penguin Ireland, 25 St Stephen's Green, Dublin 2, Ireland (a division of Penguin Books Ltd)
Penguin Group (Australia), 707 Collins Street, Melbourne, Victoria 3008, Australia
(a division of Pearson Australia Group Pty Ltd)
Penguin Books India Pvt Ltd, 11 Community Centre, Panchsheel Park, New Delhi – 110 017, India
Penguin Group (NZ), 67 Apollo Drive, Rosedale, Auckland 0632, New Zealand
(a division of Pearson New Zealand Ltd)
Penguin Books (South Africa) (Pty) Ltd, Block D, Rosebank Office Park, 181 Jan Smuts Avenue,
Parktown North, Gauteng 2193, South Africa

Penguin Books Ltd, Registered Offices: 80 Strand, London WC2R 0RL, England

www.penguin.com

First published in Penguin Books 2013
001

Set in 11.75/15pt Baskerville MT Std
Typeset by Jouve (UK), Milton Keynes
Printed in England by Clays Ltd, St Ives plc

ISBN: 978-1-846-14529-2

www.greenpenguin.co.uk

MIX
Paper from
responsible sources
FSC
www.fsc.org  FSC™ C018179

Penguin Books is committed to a sustainable
future for our business, our readers and our planet.
This book is made from Forest Stewardship
Council™ certified paper.

ALWAYS LEARNING                    PEARSON

# I

The first District Line train out of Upminster in the morning is the first train anywhere on the Underground network. It leaves the depot at 4.53, the only train anywhere in the system to set out from its base before 5 a.m. That's a kind of record: if you catch that train, you might be tempted to say, Ta-dah! – except you probably wouldn't, because nobody is thinking Ta-dah! at seven minutes to five in the morning, certainly nobody on this train. People look barely awake, barely even alive. They feel the same way they look; I know because, this morning, I'm one of them.

I've lived in London for more than quarter of a century now, and this is the first time I've ever been on the day's first train. It's something I'd often wondered about, though, from both a practical and a romantic point of view. The practical question was a simple one: if the transport network isn't running in the early morning, how do the people who operate it get to work? How does the driver get to the train, if there are no trains to take him there?[1] The

---

1. I say him, because it's usually a him: the last figures I've seen are from 2003, when 167 out of 3,000 Underground drivers were women. And that, by the way, was after a recruitment drive targeting them. The first woman train driver on the Underground, Hannah Dadds, only started driving trains in 1978 – on the District Line, as it happens, where she had already worked for nine years, first as a ticket collector and then as a guard. That was the sequence for working your way up: ticket collector, guard, driver. Hannah qualified as a driver at her first attempt, not without encountering a certain amount of sexism en route. Then, at the age of fifty-three, as she had always planned to do, she took early retirement and went to live in Spain.

answer is prosaic: they get there by minicab. The cabs travel a prescribed route to the various depots on the District Line, picking up staff en route as they head to Upminster, Earl's Court, Ealing Common, Barking and Hammersmith. Of these postings, Upminster is the most popular, because a large number of drivers live nearby – that's one of the reasons it is, as I was told by a District veteran, the 'senior depot'. 'When a driver gets to Upminster,' he said, 'they don't leave it except in a box.' That's putting it a little melodramatically, because most of them don't leave it in a box, they just retire: but the point is, once drivers are based at leafy Upminster, they don't leave to go and work out of another depot. The first-train issue is a part

---

That story, of the girl from the East End who grew up to be a train driver and took early retirement to Spain, is like a short novel about how Britain changed in the twentieth century. Dadds died of cancer in 2011 at the age of seventy, but not before being invited to the first Women of Achievement lunch at Buckingham Palace in 2004.

of it: one of the drivers I spoke to lived near Upminster for family reasons, but was working shifts from the depot at Earl's Court. The first train out from Earl's Court in the morning is at 5.21, but to get there, allowing for multiple pick-ups and waiting around at the depot, the minicab from the East End starts its pick-ups at 2.30 in the morning. That's an early start to a working day.

The romantic side of the first train is harder to define. It's something to do with the secret nightlife of the city, the London that is carrying on while the rest of London fidgets in its sleep. There's a romance attending on those jobs, the ones which keep things running all night long: it's part of the fascination of big cities, that sense that something is always going on somewhere, even in the smallest of small hours. Bakers and police and nurses and cab drivers and market porters all belong to that secret city, the one which rumbles along so late it starts to get early. Once or twice, carrying on a long evening by going to the place after the place

I started, and then to the place after that, I've ended up in versions of this super-late or super-early London. I remember once, back in the days when journalism was wilder than it is now, ending up in the place-after-the-place-after-the-place with a group of sports desk colleagues: a packed Greek taverna, surrounded by people howling for more retsina, waiters swerving between tables carrying platters of burnt meat, the room not merely loud but roaring, and looking at my watch to see that it was quarter to four in the morning – and the point which struck me was that everyone around seemed to regard that as perfectly normal.

That was my romantic version of the first train: that it was populated by inhabitants of this Baudelairean secret London. The truth is more prosaic, and it becomes clear, not so much at Upminster, since, after all, Upminster is a relatively posh suburb, out past the East End where things are starting to feel vaguely, suburbanly rural. No, it's a few stops before you realize who these people getting on the train are, bone-tired but indefatigable: they are cleaners. By Dagenham East, a few minutes after 5 a.m., the first train on the network is already packed, and the people with whom it is packed are cleaners on their way to work. That's the unromantic truth about this version of the secret city. Once you get past Temple, the train starts to thin out again, because the people who live in the East are going to work in the financial district; the trip to work goes from out to in. Nobody commutes from Sloane Square out to Hammersmith, or from Westminster to Richmond. Once the District train gets past the City, it's practically empty, the emptiest it's been at any point on the journey so far today. Then the train gets to Richmond and turns around to head back the other way, except this time it's carrying not poor people who are going to clean offices, but much richer people on their way to early-starting jobs in the financial sector.

This is one of the realities of the District Line: the immense social and geographical and demographic range of its network, from far out in the poor East of the city to far out in the rich West. The very rich West. According to the Department of Work and Pensions, Richmond, at one western end of the line, is the most affluent borough in London. It looks like it and feels like it, too – airy, leafy, parky, rivery. Richmond has more of the richest London wards than any other borough. Mick Jagger lives there and Zac Goldsmith is the local MP. It's even too posh to be south of the river; it's the river which goes south instead, and Richmond is to the east of it. At the other western end of the District Line is Wimbledon – now, that's not much less fancy than Richmond. It has villas, it has the Common, which isn't in the least bit common, it has the All England Lawn Tennis and Croquet Club and the world's most famous tennis championships. Like Richmond, it is a suburb which is sufficiently posh, sufficiently grand, that it can also regard itself as a free-standing, desirable destination of its own: people who live there can choose between saying that 'I live in Richmond/ Wimbledon' and 'I live in London', and both sentences would be true.

At the other end of the line, that's not the case. The East is visibly poorer, poorer in ways you can see out of the train window: blocks of flats instead of houses, and the train, rather than riding above them as it often does out in the leafy West, is mostly at their level or slightly below.

I've never lived in East London – North, West and South, yes, but East, no. If I were twenty years younger that probably wouldn't be true, since London has taken a big step eastwards, not just in financial services, but also in the creative industries and the demographics which follow them. That's mainly to do with property prices, whose effect reminds me of those maps we used to look at during the Cold War, when everyone was terrified of the prospect of nuclear annihilation. They used to show maps of cities with a bull's-eye in the middle to show where the bomb had dropped, and then circles radiating outwards to show the effects of the bomb: everyone here killed instantly by the blast, everyone there fried by radiation, everyone there getting sick and dying weeks later, everyone here feeling a bit peaky and upset by the end of the world and everything, but apart from that, fine.

The effect of the rise in property prices in London has been a bit like that. The people who used to live in the middle – in places like Knightsbridge or Fitzrovia or Chelsea – now live some distance from it, in places like Clapham or Islington or Notting Hill. The people who used to live there now live further out, in places like Tooting or Hackney or Willesden; and the people who used to live there now live at almost unimaginable distances from the centre of the city, in, I don't know, Croydon or Arnos Grove, places where the Zone 1 and 2 people in the middle of the city will never avoidably go. If it's carried on for long enough, this process risks eventually turning London into Zurich, a boring and antiseptic city where everybody works in finance and there is no social variety, no diversity, no crunchiness. In some areas, in the rich parts of town, that has already happened – but that's by no means true everywhere, and it's certainly not true out in the East. The East is where immigrants tend to go, and has been since the Huguenot weavers first arrived there, to be succeeded by the Jews, the Bengalis, and all the other new arrivals. In a sense, the young creative types who are now colonizing the East End – the nearer, inner bits of it anyway – are the latest manifestation of this process. They are internal immigrants, driven east at first by the fact that they couldn't afford to live anywhere else, but then so many of them went there that they started to become a gravitational mass of their own, exerting their own attractive force, and now those bits of the East End – in District Line terms, I'm talking about Whitechapel and a few stops further out – have undergone a partial arts-led gentrification. No, that's the wrong word, since this part of town doesn't feel gentrified: artsification, maybe, since so much of the art business has now located out East too. (Make no mistake, in modern London art really is a business.) Add the younger section of the finance community who like to live close to work, and the section of the advertising world which has moved out East, first for reasons of cheapness and second for reasons of cool and critical mass, and then add the internet professions who are there for the same reasons, and then add to that the vast impact of the new developments at and around Canary Wharf, an entirely self-conscious and deliberate attempt to move the centre of gravity of London out towards the East, and it all adds up to a whole new London out beyond Whitechapel. (And this is before the impact of the Olympics, which wags in other parts of the city call the Stratford Olympics.)

But that's not what strikes me most about the East London you see from the District Line – it's not the new, artsified, moneyfied East that you see. To me, the East seems like the oldest bit of the city. Perhaps this is a way of talking about the fact that this is the part of the city where you feel most strongly the presence of the white working class. There's such a huge amount written and spoken about London as a city of diversity and immigration, of twenty-first century newness, of London as a capital of fashion and finance and football, that you forget that its largest demographic is still what it always was, the indigenous white working class. That fact is made easier to forget by the geographical displacement I've just mentioned: the indigenous working classes, more than any other group, are the ones who have been displaced by the money bomb which landed on London in the last few decades. They have been pushed out from the centre of the city by the force of money, but they're still here, further out, and especially so when you head out further east past the new moneyfied/artsified East End. This part of the city hasn't yet been airbrushed by money like so much of the rest of the capital, but I don't think that fully explains that sense of oldness, something Angela Carter remarked when she wrote an amazing paragraph, in the course of reviewing Iain Sinclair's book, *Downriver*:

I never went to Whitechapel until I was 30, when I needed to go to the Freedom Bookshop (it was closed). The moment I came up out of the Tube at Aldgate East, everything was different to what I was accustomed to. Sharp, hard-nosed, far more urban than what I was used to. I felt quite the country bumpkin, slow-moving, slow-witted, come in from the pastoral world of Clapham Common, Brockwell Park, Tooting Bec. People spoke differently, an accent with clatter and spikes to it. They focused their sharp, bright eyes directly on you: none of that colonialised, transpontine, slithering regard. The streets were different – wide, handsome boulevards, juxtaposed against bleak, mean, treacherous lanes and alleys. Cobblestones. It was an older London, by far, than I was used to. I smelled danger. I bristled like one of Iain Sinclair's inimitable dogs. Born in Wandsworth, raised in Lambeth – Lambeth, 'the Bride, the Lamb's Wife', according to William Blake – nevertheless, I was scared shitless the first time I went to the East End.

That's it. The East feels different. That might be to do with the fact that this part of London is the one which most directly bears the impact of the Second World War. The East End was very heavily bombed during the Blitz, and a large section of its population was moved further out eastwards to this further-flung part of the East – and maybe that's the thing which gives this part of the city its character: it's the last part of London where you still strongly see the impact of the war. Out and beyond Dagenham East the other ends of the line at Richmond and Wimbledon, and the version of London they exemplify, feel a long way away.

I asked TfL workers about the demographic difference between the two ends of the line. 'Put it like this,' one of them said. 'If they're annoyed about something, at this end of the line' – we were at Dagenham – 'they yell at you. You know about it straight away. At the other end,' he said with a shudder, 'they write *letters*.'

# 2

People sometimes say that London is a city of villages. A less genteel way of putting it is to say that London is a city of suburbs. The truth is somewhere in the middle: London is a city of suburbs which prefer not to use the term. That's for reasons to do with class, I suppose, and the idea that there is something inherently semi-provincial, something ineradicably lower-middle-class, about being suburban. But places like Clapham (where I live), and Notting Hill and Islington and Stoke Newington are certainly suburbs, even if they prefer not to think about themselves as suburban. The other way of looking at them, though, the old-fashioned idea that London is a city of linked villages, is not entirely wishful thinking, and you experience it in particular if you do a kind of walk that people in London, in practice, don't often do: a longish one in a straight line.

If you go on one of those walks, you notice the way the city clusters and then spreads out. It's a pattern you see all over town: large number of houses, couple of estates, cluster of shops, blank bit, more houses and estates and shops, another blank bit, repeat as before. One of the simplest ways of registering it is to do with pubs: the residential clusters have pubs, then you're in a publess middle stretch, then you're back in the world of houses-and-pubs. From where I'm sitting here, if I walk into the middle of the city, I go through Clapham, Stockwell, Kennington and then Waterloo, and all of them have that rhythm of cluster-and-gap. This is where the village nature of London is still present, in that rhythm of places, and then the spaces in between the places. It's part of what Iris Murdoch was capturing in her deathless line from her first novel, *Under the Net*: 'some parts of London are necessary, and others are contingent'.

The single biggest influence on that rhythm of place and space was the Underground. Not all of the suburbs were created by the Underground, but many were, not just in the famous Metro-land of the Metropolitan Line, but in places such as West Kensington, which was an Underground station before it was a place; or Morden, say, which was built, according to *London's Underground Suburbs* by Dennis Edwards and Ron Piagram, for 'great housing estates' which didn't yet exist. The Underground's historic role was to make these non-places into real places, to give them extra mass, to make them one of the centres of the new, spreading, densening city.

There is a little-known law on the statute books which makes it a legal requirement for every single thing ever written about the Underground to mention Harry Beck's map of the network. The fame of this map is well deserved, since it is a wondrous piece of design and a masterwork in the visual delivery of complicated information; but the map's fame has also led to it being, in a subtle but consequential way, misleading. The iconic map looks as if it is something placed down on the city from above: you can sense the city underneath it; the city, which is, as everyone knows, inaccurately represented in the clear colours and sharp angles of Beck's diagram. That makes it seem, subliminally but powerfully, as if the city was there before the map. It implies that London was an underlying reality on which the map was superimposed.

But it wasn't like that. Instead of the map being something superimposed on the city, the map created the city. Or rather, the Underground did. That's the point to stress: that London as it exists today would not be the same place without the Underground. The Underground is what gave the city its geographical spread, its population growth, its clusters of spaces and places. The new Underground stations became the places around which the city grew: they were the first gravitational mass, like the clusters of debris in the nascent solar system, which agglomerated and grew and thickened and became the planets. The Underground stations in the early years of the network were these initial clusters of mass. A 1907 photograph of Golders Green – today a thrivingly busy suburb, a traffic perma-jam and a transport hub – show next to nothing around the single-storey Underground station, except, tellingly, a couple of forlorn horse-taxis waiting to take travellers the last mile or two home. These early commuters had a journey to work which involved taking first the horse-and-cart to the station, and then the train to work. The suburb of Golders Green itself – what we today think of as the place – doesn't exist. The growth of the city created the need for a new transport network; and the growth of that network became fundamental to the growth of the city. London created the

Underground, and then the Underground created London.

This, I think, is the crucial thing to realize about the early history of the Underground, and its impact on London. The relationship between the city and the network was symbiotic. They grew together. In 1850, London was the biggest city in the world. It had a population of two and a half million. London had grown sharply to get to that point, and the pressures created by that growth were what had caused wild dreamers to begin to think of crazy solutions to its permanently jammed, reeking, barely functioning roads. (So very different from today.) The crazy solution they thought of was that of sticking trains in tunnels under the city. It is important to stress, as Christian Wolmar, Britain's leading railway historian, does in his brilliant book *The Underground Railroad*, the earliness of this venture; its daring, which verged so closely on recklessness. The next city to put in an Underground railway was Paris, and that took nearly four decades more – thirty-seven years, with the Metro opening its first lines in 1900.[2] By the standards of the technology-obsessed, innovation-crazed late nineteenth century – at least as interested in innovation as we are today, with technologies fully comparable to the Internet in their impact – thirty-seven years was an enormous gap in time, and testifies to just how far out, how advanced, the Underground idea was. Perhaps the closest

2.  There were some interesting differences when they got round to starting the Paris Metro, most of them in the traditional French direction of increased rationality and systematization. The Metro was a system of lines, a network, right from the start, rather than an opportunistic set of separate ventures. Nine lines were present from the inception; and the idea was that the network would be arranged so that no one in central Paris would ever be more than 500 metres from a Metro station. To this day there are many parts of central London that are far further from the Underground than that. It's still the case that the Metro feels more coherent and thought-through than the Underground. But it was the Underground which came first, and by a big margin.

contemporary analogy is to the Apollo landings, which were so far ahead of their time, and so risky, that forty-two years after man last walked on the moon, we are still nowhere near repeating the feat.

Unlike the Apollo landings, however, the creation of the Underground was the opposite of a historical dead end. Instead, it was so successful that the already rapid expansion of the city sped up, and by 1910 London had a population of seven million – still the biggest city in the world, only much bigger. Instead of the scattered city of suburb-villages, it was well on the way to being the place it is today, where the suburb-villages are buried in one of the planet's most formidable urban agglomerations. It was the Underground which enabled that degree of growth at that degree of speed.

The process hasn't stopped. The Underground is still shaping London's geography – perhaps especially, now, its social geography. I've been living in the same house for fifteen years, and have noticed that in the last decade or so the area around us has filled up with people who work in the financial services industry, but I didn't understand why until one day I had an appointment to meet someone at Canary Wharf. I used to work in Docklands, briefly and about twenty years ago (in a building which was subsequently blown up by the IRA). Back in those days, the commute, which featured a bus, an Underground train and the Docklands Light Railway, was grim. That time, I went there on the new (or, by then, newish) Jubilee Line and suddenly saw why there were now bankers all around where I lived: it took twenty minutes, door to door, and there I was on the huge concourse outside the enormous, capitalist-triumphalist, Norman Foster Underground station, the one with a shopping mall right there on the main concourse below ground. A belated lightbulb lit up. I realized that it was the Underground which was determining the identity of my neighbours, as surely as it has been doing for Londoners for the last 150 years.

We should, I think, think more about this

aspect of the Victorians: the scale of what they did. For instance, it's possible to imagine a counter-factual version of London which doesn't develop the Underground network. That's a smaller city, and probably one which is both more compact and more spread out – with a denser middle, and then people commuting from further afield. This alterna-London has a fairly narrow historical window in which to develop an Underground network, because once the car becomes ubiquitous, the idea of the city changes to accommodate it. Everywhere else in the world waited until electrification before developing their Underground railway networks. That makes sense, really, because when you think about it, there was something crazily reckless about the idea of running nineteenth-century steam trains, fired by coal, through tunnels under the city. Not long after that, the car arrived, and began to shape the world in its image. London might well have gone from a patchy network of, say, trams, to a wholescale submission to the car, in the way that Birmingham did. Once a city has hit a certain size and density, it becomes very difficult to create an Underground network – Hong Kong's unromantically named 'mass transit', which began being built in the late seventies, was one very successful example, but its creation was a huge struggle and might not have been possible in a democratic society, where the voices arranged against the cost and disruption would have been louder. And sometimes, darker forces are at work. Los Angeles is notoriously an example of a city in total submission to the car, without any useful form of metro network – and it didn't get that way by accident. The motor industry fought for decades to prevent the creation of any public-transport alternatives to the car: the result is a city with petrol-based transport in its DNA.

Some version of that could have happened to London, if it hadn't been not just for the technical abilities of the Victorian engineers, but also for Victorian morale. That's my term for it, anyway: for their ability to embark on projects which, as the word suggests, projected – projected their energies and ambitions over space and, even more importantly, over time. Their pomposities and deludednesses and hypocrisies and class-race-gender derangements are easy to see and to deplore at this distance, but their great strength, that ability to look forward into the future and aim their wills forward to shape it, is something we can learn from still. The thought that we can collectively act to shape the future for the better – without that, we would be lacking many things, and one of those things would be the Underground, and, as a corollary, London in its current form. It is salutary (in the dictionary sense of good for the health) and chastening (in the dictionary sense of making you feel a little bit told-off) to think about how much of the basic things that make London function as a city were built by the Victorians. My house was built by them – in fact, the whole street I live in; that's not true for all Londoners, but it is true that our sewage and water come through pipes the

Victorians built, and the network of underground pipes which makes London possible, bringing power and heat and light, water and gas and electricity, is still fundamentally Victorian. (Brixton's Electric Avenue, about a mile from where I live, isn't just the subject of a great Eddy Grant song: it was also first electrified street in the city, first plugged in and switched on in 1880.) It goes almost without saying that the Victorians built my local Underground station, Clapham Common, which opened in 1900. To an extent so great that it's hard to fully take in, we are still living in a city that the Victorians made. What, I wonder, are we doing now, which will be as essential, as useful and taken for granted any and every single day, as the things they made? What might we be able to dream up, and then to do, that would match the impact of the shabby, creaking, patchwork, Underground?

# 3

In 1974, Jonathan Raban published his first
book, a study of the psychological texture of
urban life with the memorable title *Soft City*.
All city dwellers have a soft city, a version of
the place they live imprinted inside them.
We adopt the city where we live, and the city
adopts us. That gives the city a presence inside
us, a role in our inner landscape, and that
role if anything grows deeper over time, as
we accumulate more and more memories and
experiences. This soft city is where we live, as
much as the actual physical place.

The soft city can be a story, a version of

events with a beginning and middle and end.
In the case of the Underground, however, I
don't think that's how it works. I've been living
in London for more than twenty-five years,
and I have by default, or osmosis, become a
Londoner. I have no real memory of how that
happened. For the first few years I really disliked
the place, and lived here only because it was
where I had to be for work. The city crept up
on me. I could make a story of that, I suppose,
but I can't see a way of making a story out of
my relationship with the Underground. That's
because it isn't a story with a beginning, middle
and end, but a series of fragments. This, I think,
applies to all Underground users. Commuting
to work in the morning is a completely different
experience from catching a train across town
to go and see an art exhibition; coming home
from the West End after going to a movie or
theatre or restaurant is a different experience
from travelling to a football match at a weekend,
or heading out on a first date, or going to a
hospital appointment that you're dreading.

A teenager going to Westfield on their own for the first time is having a wholly different experience from a knackered commuter heading home after work.

It's not just that the network is full of different people using it at different times of the day for different purposes – that's only to be expected. What makes it difficult to tell the story of the soft Underground – the version of the network which all its users carry in their own personal version of the soft city – is that we experience it, ourselves, in so many different states of being. My very first day at work in the city, my first day as a Londoner, I took the Underground – indeed, the District Line, from Parson's Green, before changing to take the Circle from Earl's Court to Euston Square. (The featureless office block above the station there was at that point the headquarters of MI5.) I don't remember anything about that trip except my own feelings of excitement and trepidation and a strong sense that a new part of my life was about to start. That's one Underground experience, one part of the soft city; what does it have to do with the version of me a few years later, rumbling home from a night out at the pub, half-cut? Or the version of me who used to spend Saturdays going to deliberately out-of-the-way football matches: Wimbledon at Plough Lane, Leyton Orient at Leyton (actually, now that I think about it, I only ever went to Orient for midweek evening games, for reasons I now can't even vaguely recall), or Millwall at New Cross (they were playing Tottenham, and the fans' chant was 'Gascoigne takes it up the arsehole, Gascoigne takes it up the arsehole, Gascoigne takes it up the arsehole, because he's just a Northern cunt', to the tune of 'Mine Eyes Have Seen the Glory of the Coming of the Lord'.) I took the Piccadilly Line to Hammersmith to visit my wife when she was sick in Charing Cross Hospital, and I took the Northern Line to Tooting to visit my mother when she was in St George's Hospital, where she eventually died. Some of those journeys are scarred into my memory, but they are juxtaposed with plenty of other Underground travel which I don't remember at all, which I did on a kind of autopilot – get on train, thinking about something else, travel, get off train, thinking about something else, and arrive at B, barely able to remember how I got there from A. What do all these different experiences of the Underground have to do with each other? What's the story told by this version of the soft city? I would argue that there isn't one – there is no master-narrative here, no overarching plot line connecting all the different meanings that the Underground has across a user's lifetime. You can't sum it up, and you can't make a story out of it either: it's a series of fragments.

Here is one of my fragments. There's a word I haven't used once so far in this book, a word which doesn't exactly sum up my relationship with the Underground, but which does compress into itself quite a bit of the story – my story, anyway. It's a word which crops up often in more or less every piece of writing about the

Underground. I wonder if you can guess what the word is? Here it comes: Tube.

That, for me, was once a very charged word, because I wasn't fully clear what it meant. Growing up abroad, I had heard that in London they had something called the Underground, and I knew what it was, more or less. But there was also this other thing, more modern-sounding and cooler-sounding, called the Tube. Except, was it really another thing, or a different name for the same thing? I remember wondering about this, and at the same time feeling, strongly feeling, that it would be too embarrassing to ask – this was just something you were supposed to know. Childhood is full of these gaps, the things you don't know which you know that you should – or you suspect that you should, and also you suspect that you're missing out by not knowing, but at the same time it's too exposing to just come out and ask. So that was Phase One: not knowing exactly what the Tube was.

The next phase was when I did come to know

what the Tube was. I did this by coming to London often enough, and by hanging out with Londoners enough, to learn that they use Tube and Underground interchangeably. The Tube isn't even slang, it's just the other term by which people know the Underground network. The name is quasi-official, and crops up even in ads and notifications and posters used by Transport for London, the body that runs it. So the verdict was now in: Tube = Underground.

Then I became a Londoner myself, and all of a sudden I was the person talking about the Tube, and using it in the super-casual way we do. Let's get there by Tube, it'll be quicker by Tube, the bloody Tube was running late, I hate the Tube in rush hour, how far is it from the Tube? And there, if you'd asked me, I would have said this journey ends, because I'd gone native, was using the terms Tube and Underground interchangeably, and there was nowhere else for the story to go.

Now, however, and thanks to researching this book, I know better. That's because among students and aficionados of the Underground, as well as among its staff, there is indeed a distinction, quite an important one, between the Underground and the Tube. It's a distinction I first came across in the writing of Christian Wolmar, and it is based on the fact that the first Underground lines were not tubes; that's because they were not, in the strict sense, tunnels. A tunnel is a hole that goes into the ground at one end, goes along for a bit, and then comes out at the other end – yes? But that's not how the first Underground lines were made. They were made using the 'cut and cover' method: not a tunnel, but a hole dug straight down into the ground, laid with tracks and brick walls, and then covered back up. All the first lines were 'cut and cover' lines: the Metropolitan, beginning in 1863, then the District, which opened in 1868, then the Circle, which opened in 1884. The 'cut and cover' lines are not deep: barely thirty feet below ground, and with many sections in which the line is still open to the sky, as indeed are quite a few of the stations. On these lines you can – in recognition of the fact that even in the tunnel sections you aren't that far underground – often get a mobile-phone signal. (When you do have one, it's fun to look up Google Maps from below the earth.) Those of us who don't love the sensation of being deep underground prefer the 'sub-surface' lines, as TfL calls the lines built by the cut-and-cover method: the District, the Circle and the Metropolitan. These do have stretches of genuine tunnel in them, the longest being between Notting Hill and High Street Kensington, 400-plus yards, with a vent open to the air near Camden Hill Square; but that's nothing like the extended immersion in under-London provided by the Tube lines.

The Tube was made using a fundamentally different digging technique, one pioneered by the father-and-son team of Marc and Isambard Kingdom Brunel,[3] and then perfected by Marc's

3. Marc Isambard Brunel went by the name Isambard in his lifetime, but historians prefer to call him Marc to distinguish him from his son. Bill Gates Sr, the respected

student James Greathead. It features a shield, a huge frame, on which the twelve 'navigators' who dug the tunnels stood: the frame advanced gradually through the earth while the men dug, and then other navigators bricked up the tunnel walls and roof behind them as they went. The first of these tunnels ran from Rotherhithe to Wapping, and today is part of the East London overground line, though its initial purpose was for horse and foot traffic only. (It's one of the network's many historical quirks that the first tunnel under the Thames is technically part of the overground.) Construction, which began in 1825 and took two decades, ran wildly over budget, with immense difficulties and several deaths. The technology and the new techniques learned were more important than the tunnel itself turned out to be. This was the birth of the Tube: the deep tunnels

---

corporate lawyer whose son is the more famous Bill Gates, has said that he would give his son a different name if he had the choice over again.

which were dug using the shield technique, and which run through the clay subsoil underneath London, are in the strict sense the Tube. The Underground includes the Tube, but the Tube does not include the Underground. This means that, now that I've become an Underground nerd, I've gone back to using the word Underground and Tube separately, because the distinction is so useful. My ten-year-old self, without knowing it, was on to something: the Underground and the Tube are not the same thing.

In my view, the main reason why the distinction is useful is because the experience of using the Tube lines is, for people who don't love the sensation of being deep underground, more challenging than it is on the sub-surface lines. I can testify to this from frequent personal experience, because the Underground station nearest me is Clapham Common. That means that the line I use most often is a Tube line, the Northern, oldest of all of them: it began life as the City and South London Line, on which work began in 1886. The Northern Line is sometimes called the 'Misery Line', though it could equally fairly be described as one of the wonders of the world, given that it for years was the world's longest train tunnel, disappearing into the earth at Morden and then not popping up above ground again until Finchley, seventeen and a half miles later.

I don't love tunnels at the best of times: there have been stretches of my life when that was a proper phobia, a powerful, irrational fear, and other stretches when it was no more than a mild aversion, which is what it is at the moment. Many, many people share this feeling, about which they are usually reluctant to speak, for reasons of embarrassment which I fully share. It is an uncool thing to admit to, being scared of the Tube. For myself, I can actually date the moment the dislike began: 9 p.m. on 18 November 1987. I was in the bath, getting ready to go out later that evening, when the phone rang. It took me a moment to summon up the strength to get out of the water and

answer, but I was glad I did, because I was
greeted by my mother's voice saying, as soon
as I picked up the receiver, 'Thank God!' She
had been watching the *Nine O'Clock News*, whose
lead item was a fire at King's Cross Station.
I lived a couple of hundred yards away, and
used the station every day, a fact my mother
well knew. After I got off the phone I opened
the window, and could immediately smell
the damp smoke in the aftermath of the fire.
Thirty-one people died that day: in response,
the Underground began its journey back from
decades of underinvestment and neglect; and,
a fact which has no consequence for anyone but
me, I've never since felt quite the same about
being on a stationary train deep underground.

The issue with the Northern Line, for the
tunnel-averse, is not so much its length, because
hardly anyone except the driver travels the
full length of the line, but its narrowness. The
various technological and engineering constraints
around the construction of the Tube – basically,
the fact that it was an extraordinarily difficult

and daring thing to do – put severe constraints on the size of the tunnels. At the start, they were a mere 10 foot, 6 inches in diameter; they were then widened, but they're still no more than 11 foot, 8½ inches, which is, I find when I start to think about it, unsettlingly narrow. My discomfort with that fact kicks in not so much when the train is in motion as when it stops in the middle of tunnels. If that happens on the deep Tube lines, I'm not a happy bunny.

When the train comes to a halt, there's a sensation of airlessness which is particularly uncomfortable because the deep Tube trains don't have air conditioning (and because of technical constraints, on most lines, never will – again, it's those narrow tunnels which are to blame). In summer, that means that the heat builds up fast, with no air movement to give a faint sense of relief. Even when the trains are running, temperatures on a hot day can get over 35°C. I mention that figure because it is the legal limit for the transportation of livestock.

You can't legally truck cattle in it, but you can move people around on the Underground – except, of course, when the train comes to a halt. Then, the temperatures can rise so quickly that there is soon no other course of action possible except to evacuate the train. A driver told me that in his experience of the deep Tube on a hot summer day that can happen within twelve minutes. And then what happens? You are led out through the front of the train, as follows: the power in the line is turned off, the lights in the tunnel come on, a section of the driver's cab opens out forwards, he puts down a ladder, and he escorts the passengers out the front of the train down the track towards the next station. One driver I spoke to had had to do this twice in his career, and he was very matter-of-fact about it, but it did leave me thinking that I wished I didn't know one single detail in particular: the fact that the deep Tube tunnels are so narrow you can't get out of the side of a stuck train, but have to exit through the front.

On the sub-surface lines, none of this feels as if it matters nearly as much. This is an irrational belief, of course, since being stuck in a tunnel is being stuck in a tunnel, but there's a component of the shallower depth which makes it easier to take. The cut-and-cover tunnels are more spacious than the Tube tunnels, and they have frequent junctions and intersections where the tunnels open out into each other. Early illustrations of the Metropolitan Line, drawn to entice wary customers into the smelly, smoky, steamy tunnels, are hilariously spacious and airy, and barely hint at the trains being underground. OK, the sub-surface lines are not really like that – but they're more like that than the deep Tube.

And then there is the crucial, defining fact that the sub-surface lines have sections which aren't underground at all. The Tube is a tube, but the Underground is by no means all underground. Only 45 per cent of the whole network runs through tunnels. The figure is even lower on the District Line. In total, only about a third of the line runs through tunnels, and if you take the train the full length of the line, from Upminster to Richmond or the other way around, you are made strongly aware of the fact that the tunnel section is no more than an interlude. Of the sixty stations on the line, thirty-five are on sections which are above ground (and this is leaving out places such as Earl's Court and South Kensington, where the station is open to the sky, but there are tunnels at either end of the platform). The train starts in one set of suburbs, the posh West or the rougher East, both of them above ground, and only dives underneath the city when it comes into the super-built-up, expensive middle of town. Property prices force the train underground, into the dark and the tunnels, where a significant portion of the people on the train are spending a significant amount of emotional energy on trying not to think about what happens if the train comes to a halt.

# 4

The Underground lines are different in character. You'd expect that: they go to different places and they have different demographics, histories, physical characteristics, trains, everything. One thirty-year veteran of the Underground told me that the Piccadilly, where he began his career, 'is a floozy. Whereas the District Line is like an old aunt who's seen better days.' That may change before long: 2015 will see the arrival of new, dramatically more modern S-stock trains and the shift to a new control centre at Earl's

Court: the second of those developments may pass unnoticed, but even the most oblivious District Line commuter will spot the new trains, and find them shinier and more modern than the D-stock trains that entered service in 1980. Will that make the line feel less aunt-like? Probably not – any network which runs between Putney and Dagenham is never going to feel too dangerous and cutting-edge. But she may come to feel like a younger, cooler, more tech-savvy aunt.

The aunt-like qualities of the District Line have a strong basis in history. Another way of describing them is to say, as a manager at the Baker Street control centre did, that the line is 'more of a patchwork quilt than the other lines' – a metaphor he used a few times. That attribute comes from the history of the line. It's the second oldest after the Metropolitan Line, and in its early years was known as the Metropolitan District, a designation which was eventually simplified to District on 1 July 1933 because a) it was confusing and b) the managements of the two organizations hated each other. It began operation on 24 December 1868,[4] as a short section between Westminster Bridge (Westminster, as the station now is) and South Kensington, with intermediate stops at St James's Park, Victoria Station (an important one, because it opened up access to the overground railway networks), Sloane Square and South Kensington. At South Ken the

4. The line opened on Christmas Eve because Christmas Day was going to be so busy – a historic irony, since that is now the only day of the year when the whole Underground network is closed. The only people who go into the network on that day now are graffiti artists, who use it to tag areas which would be inaccessible, or mortally dangerous, on days when the trains are running. Many of the tags are in places where only the driver can see them – a driver pointed a few of them out to me when I was travelling in the cab of his train. They were simple signatures rather than more complicated works, and there was something strange and private about the idea that these things would never be seen by anyone other than train drivers and the clean-up crews who eventually come to erase them.

new line joined end-on with the Metropolitan Line's recent extension, which had opened a few months before. This was an important first step in the attempt to build a circular line all round the capital, and an important step in the Underground system becoming a genuine network of lines – a process which would have been a lot easier if the lines hadn't spent so much time and energy fighting each other, selling mutually incompatible tickets, and so on.

There was always a bodged-together, improvised quality about the District Line. All the early Underground lines were built with a combination of private money and public legislation to let the building go through. The combination was a good one for getting railways built, but a less certain one for making them instantly profitable – though it has to be said that it was dramatically more effective than the modern equivalent, the public-private partnership, which, as Christian Wolmar points out, cost £500 million in consultancy and lawyers' fees before a single spadeful of earth was dug. The whole idea of the District was that it would run through some of the richest parts of the city. An immediate problem with that is that the richest parts of the city are also the most expensive parts, and complicated questions of where to run the line immediately ensued. The line was supposed to run along the newly constructed Thames Embankment, built by Joseph Bazalgette to incorporate an underground railway and the pipes needed to clean up the city's sewage system. The idea was for the construction of the railway and the sewer to be simultaneous, but the reality proved more complicated, and the new line often had to have separate building works, adding to both the complexity and the expense of the project.

That issue – about the expense of the real estate overhead – has always been a central factor in the history of the Underground. The cut-and-cover lines ran along roads, as much as they could, to reduce the risk of damaging the expensive houses overhead. When the people in the way were poor, it was of course far simpler to have them evicted and the buildings knocked down, but that was hardly ever true for the District Line, running as it did under expensive central London and then, later, out into the only-just-being-built suburbs. Even with the deep Tube lines, there was concern about possible damage via subsidence, and the lines often make small changes of route to avoid expensive real estate up above. Without those small changes, the lines could have run dead straight, since they were cut through the clay underneath the city and geological factors were largely irrelevant. That means that, when you're riding the Tube and it makes small shifts in direction – shifts you can hear as much as feel, through the friction of the wheels on the tracks as its momentum moves – they are being caused by the cost of the city up above you. London's history is full of themes, and one of those themes is the effect of rich people upon the city, and that's something you experience most times a Tube train does anything other than run straight.

The cost and complexity of building underground lines through a built-up metropolis will never be anything other than formidable, and in retrospect it's not surprising that the Underground was difficult to build. Over the many years of its construction, however, the complexities continued to accumulate. The Circle Line was both an aspiration and a complication: everyone could see the virtue of an Underground line linking the capital's main overground stations, but that didn't make the administrative and engineering issues any easier in practice, especially given that the competing companies hated each other. The result, today, is that 'patchwork quilt', in which the District Line on some sections runs on its own track, on other sections runs on Circle or Metropolitan Line track, and on yet others – out in the West – runs on track which is nothing to do with Transport for London, but in fact belongs to Network Rail, the national overground company. That section has a different operating system from the Underground, one in which the signalman is in charge, instead of the controller. ('I tell my drivers, the big difference is that in Network Rail, the signalman is God,' a manager told me. That's because they have far fewer trains to think about at any given moment; on the Underground, where there are trains zooming everywhere at two-minute intervals, control has to be passed to the control rooms, where they can see the overall picture of what's happening on the line.) Most of the lines just run their own trains on their own tracks, but many non-District trains run on District track, and the line has responsibility for them while they do. The District has three branches in the West, out to Ealing and Richmond and Wimbledon; a separate service from Wimbledon to Edgware, and a branch line to Olympia, which only runs during big events. The District is the only Underground line which crosses the Thames over a bridge; in fact, over two bridges, one of them, at Kew, owned by Network Rail; the other, at Putney, owned by TfL. It also runs under a river, only that river isn't the Thames, but the Westbourne, which runs through a pipe above the platform at Sloane Square. For all these reasons, the District Line, as well as being the Underground line with the biggest number of stations – sixty, is the most complicated of all the lines. 'Its complexity is second to none,' a manager told me, with audible pride.

To experience that complexity first hand, I was lucky enough to wangle a trip with a driver in the cab of a District Line train, one day in May last year. This was the fulfilment of a long-held ambition. Since the first times I rode on the Underground I've been fascinated by those brief glimpses you get into the driver's cab as the train pulls into the station. The cab looks so cosy, so self-contained, so snug and safe; a world unto itself. Everybody on the train is on their way to somewhere, often to or from work, but the driver is actually working, the only person on the train who is in the process of doing his job. On hot days, the drivers also sometimes have the door at the side of the cab open, and I've always thought there's something agreeably raffish about that – it makes the driver look like a cowboy riding on top of a horse-drawn carriage in a Western.

The experience of going out in a driver's cab more than fulfilled my long-held expectations, and a big part of that was because of the view from the front of the train, which is so much better than the passenger's normal view – rivetingly, fascinatingly, amazingly better. It's so much more involving than the normal passenger view that now when I'm on an Underground train I often find myself wishing that the passenger coaches had screens showing the view out of the front of the train, in the way that some airplanes let the passengers tune into the view from the front of the plane. (By the way, any one of us can get a glimpse of the driver's eye view, thanks to the driver's view DVDs made by a company called Video 125. When you start researching the Underground, you soon realize there's a reason why train-spotters are generally regarded as setting the gold standard for nerdy knowledgeability about a subject.[5] There doesn't seem to be a single aspect of the Underground network, or the UK train network in general, that hasn't had at least one book written about it. The DVDs which focus on trains going through tunnels are a little, what's the word, specialist in nature – I've watched the Northern Line one all the way through, and, well, let's just say it's no *Hot Tub Time Machine*. The District line DVDs – there are two, one on the central and western sections of the line, and one on the line out to the east – are more interesting, because there's a lot more to see.)

Trains show you a particular version of the urban landscape, the unpolished and undressed rear of buildings. I've always liked that about the view from the train, that you're seeing a town or city as it looks in private, before it's dolled itself up to go out, whereas the the view

5. In America, train-spotters are known as 'foamers', because of their tendency to foam with excitement.

from a car is always of the public self, putting its formal self-presentation on display. The backs of houses are always more humanly revealing than the fronts. Add to this the variety of perspectives from the District Line, from the leafy West over the Thames and through the tunnels up to Edgware or out to the East, which is first gritty, then rough, then beaten-down, then, at the last gasp, in Upminster, goes back to being leafily suburban again; add all these things together, and the view from the front is something everyone should see once.

The view is another one of the reasons why drivers prefer to work on the District, and why Upminster is, as I've already said, the senior depot.

'The variation makes it much easier,' my driver told me. 'In the tunnels all you see is the dark and the signal lights. It's more tiring because there's nothing to stimulate your mind. The signals are easier to see in the dark, but that's the only advantage. I used to work on the Bakerloo. On that line, in winter, you get up in the dark, spend your whole day in tunnels in the dark, and then go home in the dark. The District is more pleasant to work on, a lot more interesting.'

I can believe that without difficulty: the constantly changing view from the front would be, if you were the driver, one of the high spots of your working day. The moment when you go into the tunnel is a particular point of drama and interest: as you take the train from Upminster into town you see the tunnel coming towards you at Upney. For most of the above-ground section, the train tracks are, to one degree or another, raised, so the sensation of diving below the earth is even more dramatic. You can see where the expression 'tunnel vision' comes from: all you can see is the narrow black tunnel, where seconds before there was a 270-degree perspective around and in front of the cab.

In the tunnel, the signal lights stand out very brightly. I thought of all the times I'd travelled in an Underground train, completely unaware

of them, yet being ruled by their orders: red
for 'Stop'; amber meaning that the next light
ahead is red. Some lights are always red until
the train comes up to them, which explains
something I'd often noticed and wondered
about: those places where, even though there
are no trains in the tunnel ahead, and even
though there are no junctions or intersections
marked on the map, the train always comes
to a stop, or near-stop. I was surprised to feel,
given that I don't much like tunnels, that there
is something cosy and safe-feeling about being
in the tunnels when you're in the driver's cab.
Maybe that's because you are never out of
radio contact: the thick cables which carry
the Underground's communication systems
are visible all the way along the tunnel walls.
The fact that you can see ahead also makes a
big psychological difference, especially since
you can see the brightly lit stations from some
distance away – quite often, when the train is
at a halt, you can actually see the station you're
heading for just in front of you. Since the driver

knows the ropes, he knows the likely reason for having come to a halt.

One particular point where this is likely to happen on the District Line is the junction around Aldgate East, where the Circle loops round and feeds into the same section of track being used by the District; that's the second-busiest intersection on the Underground. The busiest is the 'triangle', the area in between South Kensington, Notting Hill Gate and Earl's Court, where two sets of District Line trains, from Edgware to Wimbledon and Richmond to Upminster, feed into the loop where Circle Line trains are also running. This, in my experience, is the commonest point on the entire network to get held in a tunnel – usually, it has to be said, for a fairly brief period. A line controller told me that any stop adds two minutes to the journey, because that's how long it takes the train to slow down and get back up to speed again. In the triangle, if you come to a halt to let a train go in front of you, that train will always seem to be from the other line: if you're on a Circle Line train, the driver will tell you that you're stuck behind a District, and if you're on a District train, he'll tell you that you're stuck behind a Circle. (The fact is that you're more likely to be stuck behind a District Line train, because there are twice as many of them.) This is a driver's in-joke.

I noticed that when we passed a train going the other way, the driver would wave at some, but not all, of the other drivers. Then I realized he was waving at District Line drivers and ignoring those from the Circle; nothing hostile in that, just that he knew one set of drivers from the depot, and didn't know the others. I've asked several TfL people if there are major differences in the character of the lines' workforce: I think I was hoping that the answer would be yes, and that I'd be told the drivers on one line are all unpublished poets, on another they're all ex-military, on a third they all day-trade stocks and shares in their time off . . . But that doesn't seem to be the case. The demographics of the workforce are very similar across all the Underground lines, with the slight qualification, noted earlier, that drivers as they get older sometimes graduate from the deep Tube lines to the pleasanter working conditions of the sub-surface network.

That isn't the only thing that happens as they get older. I wasn't exactly warned about this, but the issue was raised. 'The thing about the drivers,' I was told, 'is that they spend a lot of time on their own. They can get a bit cranky, especially the older ones.' I can't really comment on that, since my driver wasn't at all cranky – but I can certainly confirm the point about the isolation of the driver's job. Indeed, that was the most striking thing about it. A packed Underground train can have a thousand people on it. And yet the driver is on his own in the cab, the other side of a locked door. When he's on duty, he's completely isolated: there's no one to talk to, and the concentration required means that any of the forms of distraction and entertainment available to everybody else on the train are forbidden. No mobile phone calls, nothing to read, no music. It is as isolated a working environment as any I've ever seen. The round-trip from Upminster to Richmond and back took three hours and twenty minutes, and the only moment of variety in it was when the driver got out of the cab, locked the door, walked to the other end of the train, unlocked the door and got in the cab to begin the return journey. In the trip we took, the driver once spoke to central control, to report that one of the monitors at Whitechapel wasn't working properly, with lines flickering across its screen so that it was hard to see. Apart from that, if I hadn't been there, he wouldn't have exchanged a word with anyone in nearly three and a half hours. The announcements that are piped through the train at regular intervals – about the stops we're coming to, about disruptions on other lines, status updates and all that – are all from the line's central communications control. He himself didn't once speak to the passengers.

I once saw a television documentary about a French baker whose work involved getting up at three in the morning. 'C'est mon travail, c'est ma solitude,' he said – it's my work, it's my solitude. Being a driver on an Underground train is like that. I'm an only child and like time on my own, and since I'm a writer my work is by definition solitary, so I'm used to a solitary working context; but I would find the degree of isolation in a train driver's working life hard to get used to.

Some trains on other lines are largely automated, and all the driver does is press the Start or Stop button when going into or coming out of stations; the regulation of the train's movement is done through electronic signals transmitted through the track. (The Jubilee Line is fully automated, and could adopt driverless trains right now; the Victoria Line isn't far behind.) The new trains coming to the sub-surface lines will have this technology too: from 2015, all the trains on the network will be the new S-stock, replacing the C- and D-stock trains currently in service. (The train I went out on was D-stock, which runs on the line from Upminster to Richmond; the line also has C-stock trains, running from Edgware Road to Wimbledon. This makes it the only line which has two different sorts of train running on it, and drivers who are trained for both. All drivers have to re-pass competence tests every year.) The new kind of train can be seen already on the Metropolitan line, and it is, even to people with no interest in the subject, instantly distinguishable, because it doesn't have separate compartments: the train is open all along the inside. The effect is airier and less claustrophobic, I was told, though I'm not sure: I like the windows you can open at either end of the compartments on the existing stock. 'They're more modern,' a manager told me about the S-stock trains, 'and one of the things that means is they have fewer seats.' Seeing from my expression that I didn't regard that as an improvement, he laughed and added: 'That also means we can get more people on them.' Another improvement which seems to me more of an improvement is that the new trains will be the first on the Underground to have air conditioning. The order to Bombadier in Derby for nearly two hundred new S-stock trains is the largest single order of trains ever made. It's part of the huge upgrade coming to the entire Underground network, which, along with Crossrail – the biggest infrastructure project in Europe – will see a signifcant increase in both the capacity of the network and the pleasantness of the experience for its users.

This, however, is the District Line of the future, not of today. Here, the drivers still drive the trains: boost and cut back the engine, put on the brakes to come to a halt, watch out for signals and so on. At platforms, the driver has the responsibility for letting people off and on the train, in that order of importance. 'You try to make sure everyone gets off,' he told me. 'That's the main thing. When it's busy, you sometimes don't have time to let everyone who wants to get on a train get on, and if you do it just slows things down anyway. People sometimes behave as if it's the overground and there won't be another train along for an hour, instead of another one coming in two minutes.' He sees the passengers getting off and on via either a small bank of TV monitors, or via mirrors at the end of the platform, positioned so that the driver can watch them when he looks across from his cab.

This takes concentration and practice. The train's movement is controlled through a single handle, with four settings for forward motion and seven for slowing down. I noticed that the driver had an especially subtle touch with the brake, constantly adjusting its settings to bring the train to a stop at exactly the right spot on the platform; he was making small changes to the braking more or less all the time, and, over his decade on the trains, the work involved had become entirely internalized and unconscious. This handle, which controls the movement of the train, has to be twisted into position at right angles for the train to move at all; let go of the handle and it snaps into a vertical position. That makes the train comes to a halt. This is the famous 'dead man's handle' (a much more evocative term than the official 'driver's safety device'). The full run from Upminster in the East to Richmond in the West takes an hour and a half, and the driver's hand is clamped to the handle all that time, except when the train is in a station. I hadn't appreciated this element of physical discomfort involved in train driving – it looks like a certain recipe for arthritis or RSI.

All in all, the driving was a mixture of monotony and concentration, and although I've written about how much I enjoyed the view from the front of the train, the drivers of necessity enjoy it much less, since they're having to look out for signals. These aren't all that easy to spot, in changing light conditions: easier for the drivers, maybe, since they know where they are, but much harder than (say) traffic lights, and although the tunnels make the lights stand out far more, there are also sections where the tunnels bend and the perspectives make them quite hard to decode – you can't instantly see which is the light immediately in front of you

and which the one in the middle distance.
I don't quite know what I was expecting the job
of driving trains to look like, but it wasn't what
I found: the mixture of monotony, isolation,
concentration, responsibility and occasional
dramatic crises – my driver had twice had to walk
all the passengers on his train down switched-off
tracks to the next station. It's an unusual
job. Even the shift pattern is unusual: because
the Underground is open about nineteen hours
a day, the shifts move through the hours in a
pattern designed to avoid overly brutal jumps
between day and night work. This schedule is
set out 110 weeks in advance, so everyone can
look at the calendar for more than two years
ahead and see when they will be at work and
when they'll be having time off.

For anyone curious about what it's like
to drive an Underground train, I've already
mentioned the driver's eye DVDs which let you
see the view from the front of the train. But
for a more immersive or hands-on version of
the experience, one which lets you get to grips

with what the drivers are actually doing at the front of the train, I can recommend a video game with the catchy title, *World of Subways Volume Three: London Underground*, and no, I'm not joking. This game got a good review in *Train Sim Monthly* (still not joking) and offers you the driver's perspective of the Circle Line, all 53 kilometres and thirty-five stations of it, except here you don't just look out of the window, you take decisions about operating the train. The extraordinary graphics are deep in what nerds call the 'uncanny valley' between full realism and cartoon artificial. If you've ever been curious about what it's like to drive an Underground train, get hold of a copy and knock yourself out. Maybe best not to mention it on a first date, though.

# 5

More people use the Underground to commute than for any other single purpose. If there is one single activity which sums up people's experience of the Underground – I would argue that there isn't, but if there were – it would be commuting. This, like Tube, is another word which has been on a journey. 'Commute' in its original sense means to give something in exchange for something else, or to change one thing into another. A criminal sentence might be 'commuted' from, say, hanging, to life imprisonment. The word crossed over to use in a railway context in the USA, where regular travellers began to swap day tickets for better-value season tickets; they 'commuted' their daily tickets into season tickets. The *Oxford English Dictionary* gives the first instance of the modern, dragging-your-weary-bones-to-work sense as in the American magazine the *Atlantic Monthly*, which defined a commuter as follows: 'one who purchases a commutation-ticket'. A commutation-ticket was the American term for a season ticket. Commuters commuted 'commute'.

This kind of travel, commuting in the modern sense, was a new thing: travelling a considerable distance, there and back every day, in order to work in one place while you lived in another. This new kind of travel was to be central to the growth of the modern city, with London as the first and biggest example of its importance: the modern map of London, the modern city, was created by commuting. One of the consequences of it, gently hinted at in *The Subterranean Railway*, was that people had more sex – they moved to bigger houses, where they could sleep in separate bedrooms from their children.

Commuting is interesting and important for another reason too. It was a new kind of time in the day: an interstitial mental space between home life and work. Companies like Starbucks talk about, and try to position themselves in, what they call the 'third place', in between work and home. Commuting can be a mental form of 'third place'. It can be when people get some of their most sustained reading or thinking done, their most extended daily period of introspection or of listening to music. In order to be that, though, the commute has to be sufficiently reliable and sufficiently comfortable to not introduce extra difficulties into the day: if your commute is a source of stress and hassle, then you aren't likely to accumulate any benefit from it. My first commuting days were on the District Line, Parson's Green to Earl's Court and then Earl's Court to Euston Square, and one of the things I remember most vividly about it was that sense that it was a new thing, different from any other travel I'd ever done. My own experience was that commuting was two entirely different experiences: a packed, unpredictable, airless standing trip into work, during which it was impossible to read because there wasn't space to hold a book in front of me; then, at the other end of the day, a calmer, more reliable, often seated, reading-friendly trip home.

That less pleasant form of commuting is something which has attracted attention in the growing new field of happiness studies. People have all sorts of fantasies about what might make them happier, most of them centring on the theme of what they might do if they had more money, or had some specific material possession or other (a Porsche, a nose job, a holiday in Ibiza). By and large, these beliefs aren't valid. You quickly get used to the new state of affairs and start wanting the next thing up: having that extra £10,000 makes you want a further £10,000 on top, the Porsche makes you want a Ferrari, the nose job a boob job, the Ibiza holiday another longer Ibiza holiday. This is called 'the hedonic treadmill': we're all hamsters running on a wheel, chasing a notion of happiness which is permanently just out of reach. One of the things this finding implies is that there is something innate about people's level of happiness, a 'set point', as it's called, which varies from person to person. The hedonic treadmill means that most of the things we do don't move us far from our set point.

There are exceptions, though, and one of them concerns commuting. Modern economics bases much of its analysis on the idea that people 'maximize their utility'. The idea is that everything we do makes sense in some material way or other: the economic view of commuting would be that although people don't necessarily enjoy it, they do it to earn money which makes up for the effort in other ways. So you commute, which is a drag, in order to have the house and holiday and lifestyle which makes you happy – yes? Well, no, according to happiness studies. Cutting down on the commute is one of the few things people can do which genuinely makes them happier. That's because, according to one academic paper, 'people with longer commuting time report systematically lower subjective well-being'. In other words, a difficult commute makes people miserable in ways for which money doesn't make amends.

This is an academic finding which hasn't crossed over into the wider world. I've never seen a film or television programme about the importance of commuting in Londoners' lives; if it comes to that, I've never read a novel that captures it either. The centrality of London's Underground to Londoners – the fact that it made the city, historically, and makes it what it is today, and is woven in a detailed way into the lives of most of its citizens on a daily basis – is strangely under-represented in fiction about the city, and especially in drama. More than a billion Underground journeys take place every year, 1.1 billion in 2011, and 2012 will certainly post a larger number still: that's an average of nearly three and a half million journeys every day. At its busiest, there are about six hundred thousand people on the network simultaneously. That means that, if the network at rush hour were a place of its own – if the rush-hour network was a city to itself, rather than being an entity inside London – it would have a bigger population than Glasgow, the fourth biggest city in the UK. The District Line also carries about 600,000 people every day, which means that it, too, is a version of Glasgow.

There are quite a few novels and films and TV programmes about Glasgow. Where are the equivalent fictions about the Underground? New York has any number of films about its subway – *The Warriors*, the John Carpenter movie from 1979, is one of the best of them, one which explicitly celebrates the network's geographical reach across the whole city, from Van Cortland Park in the Bronx to Coney Island. New York also has Joseph Sargent's *The Taking of Pelham 123*, an all-subway-located thriller, among many other cinematic depictions. Paris has the Luke Besson film *Subway*, and plenty of other movies. London has next to nothing. (Let's gloss over the Gwyneth Paltrow vehicle *Sliding Doors* – though not before noting that the crucial moment when she either does or doesn't catch the train is on the District Line, at Fulham Broadway. Spoiler alert: in the version in which she rushes and successfully catches the train, she later dies. A District Line driver would point out that this is a useful reminder that this isn't the national rail network, and there will be another one along in a minute.) There's a wonderfully bad Donald Pleasance movie from 1972 called *Death Line*, set entirely in Russell Square Underground station; there were some episodes of *Doctor Who* in the sixties, which seemed scary at the time, about the Tube network being taken over by robot yetis. To a remarkable extent, though, that's it. London is at the centre of innumerable works of fiction and drama and TV and cinema, but this thing that is at the centre of London life, which does more to create the texture of

London life than any other single institution, is largely and mysteriously absent.[6]

6. *Skyfall*, which came out just after the proofs of this book came thumping down on my doormat, is a welcome addition to the filmography not just of the Underground but – hooray! – of the District Line itself. The station through which Bond chases his love interest, played by Javier Bardem – sorry, *villain*, I mean *villain* – is clearly identified as Temple, on the District, and the crowded train he then gets on is shown as a District Line train, too. Except it isn't: that isn't Temple station, and that's manifestly a train from the deep Tube lines rather than the sub-surface network. They're easy to spot because they're a different shape – the Tube trains are rounded, Tube-shaped, for obvious reasons. And there is another, more important unease in this part of the movie. Shortly afterwards, a Tube train crashes through the floor of the network and nearly kills Bond. But we can easily see that the train is empty, and nobody's life is at risk except the driver; and the driver is clearly seen flinching and ducking, but unhurt. Moments before the Underground was packed, but this train is empty? It makes no sense. The filmmakers, having evoked the routine crowdedness of the Tube, obviously felt uneasy at the prospect of killing off hundreds of commuters just for a special effect.

Why? There is one prosaic reason: it's difficult to get permission to film on the Underground. I refer back to the figures for the sheer busy-ness of the network: with getting on for three and a half million people riding on it every day, there just isn't time and space and logistical capacity for film crews to budge ordinary Londoners out of the way for long enough to do their thing. As an ordinary Londoner, I appreciate that: sometimes, in a city with so much disruption of so many different types, it seems as if the last people anyone remembers are the ordinary citizens trying to go about their ordinary business. But the restrictions on filming in the Underground do contribute to its relative absence in film and television.

There's also perhaps another, deeper reason

---

The audience would have found it just too disturbing. They wanted the crash-bang, but they needed also to signal that it was fake. The whole sequence is a fascinating exercise in the limits and difficulties of depicting the Underground on cinema.

for the absence. Londoners spend a lot of their time and energy performing themselves. The city is a kind of catwalk. I don't mean that it is that for everyone, all the time; I don't mean that that's the only thing it is. But Londoners do act out versions of themselves in public, and wear uniforms, and signal that they belong to particular tribes. Not all of this activity is conscious, but quite a lot of it is, and even when it isn't, a lot of it is easily legible. You can stand in a queue at a Starbucks and see in the line in front of you a city boy, a Sloane who has a job doing something arty, a guy working on a screenplay, a mother just back from the gym, three tourists and two policemen (mind you, they're the easy ones to spot, since they're literally wearing uniform). Everybody stays in character. The city spaces are performance spaces – people are acting out a version of themselves.

It isn't like that on the Underground. Londoners treat the Underground not as a stage set, a place where we're on display, but as a neutral space, one in which we don't overtly direct our attention at each other. People sneak glances at each other, of course they do, but the operative word is 'sneak'. They don't look openly, in the way they would elsewhere. The main focus of people's attention is inward. They go into themselves. Or they go into the world of whatever entertainment they're carrying. Once upon a time, that would mainly have been a paid-for newspaper – but nothing has disappeared as fast and as completely from the world of the Underground as the paid-for newspaper. A couple of decades ago and you would often be in a train carriage in which most of the people present were reading a paper they'd bought. Now, there won't be a single person. Many people will be reading the paper, mind you: it's just that they'll be reading free papers, the *Metro* in the morning and the *Evening Standard* in the afternoon. The old distinctions of who read what have disappeared. On the District Line, there used to be a split between the city workers, travelling west to east, who would be reading the *Financial Times*, and the East Enders, travelling east to west, who would be reading tabloids. Now it's all free papers. Drivers get a clear view of that. 'When I walk back through the train the end of the shift,' a driver told me, 'I used to see all the papers.' I asked him if he ever saw the paper I was writing for at the time. 'Not a single copy in the last two years,' he said.

There will be roughly as many people on some form of portable entertainment console or music player as there are reading the paper. I would say the split is broadly as follows: about a quarter reading a free paper, another quarter on their handheld (mainly phones and music players but the occasional gaming-only console too), fewer than a quarter reading a book and a few more than a quarter staring into inner space. While they're doing that staring, they usually look down, to make it unmistakably clear that they aren't staring at other people in the compartment. People are very careful about what they do with their eyes on the Underground.

Again, that's because the Underground is not a performance space. People don't go there to be on show, to act themselves in front of other people. They also don't like it when people do act up and act out – when somebody does that, you can feel it, the disapproval and resentment, the pulling-back. (My favourite fictional version of this is in Alan Hollinghurst's novel *The Swimming-Pool Library*, when the train stops in a tunnel, and silence descends, broken by the narrator's friend loudly asking: 'Could you ever get into spanking?') While people are on Underground trains, they go inwards, or they go somewhere else, into the world of whatever they're reading or hearing or playing.

Not everybody is scared of the Underground, but I would argue that many people, perhaps even most people, find the experience to one degree or other (to repeat the term I used earlier) to be what psychologists call 'aversive'. It's not necessarily the tunnels: it's the whole business of being crammed into such an enclosed space with so many strangers. Looking at a full train, you sometimes think: how on earth do people manage to do that? How do they talk themselves into believing that this degree of crush, of proximity, is something normal? Research into our sense of personal space suggests that the normal radius for personal distance is between arm's length and about four feet away. Closer contact than that is an intrusion into 'intimate space', which is reserved for close family members and lovers. On the Underground, though, when it's busy, that intimate space is also reserved for the sweaty man with his arm on the strap over your head, and the young woman in a tracksuit listening to dubstep through iPhone earbuds about six inches from your head, and the two suited salesmen types who, you can tell, while also wishing you couldn't, have just eaten a curry washed down with cider, and a worried and unhappy-looking middle-aged woman trying to brace herself against the compartment wall whose head is directly under your armpit. Even without being jolted along in the dark tunnel –

even without coming to a halt in a dark tunnel, for an unspecified reason, for an unspecified length of time, as the heat mounts – this is a profoundly unnatural condition for human beings. We react to it by going somewhere else in our heads. It is the inner space evoked by T. S. Eliot in 'East Coker':

> *Or as, when an underground train, in the tube,*
> *stops too long between stations*
> *And the conversation rises and slowly fades*
> *into silence*
> *And you see behind every face the mental*
> *emptiness deepen*
> *Leaving only the growing terror of nothing*
> *to think about.*

(Note the precision with which Eliot specifies that it's not any underground train, but the Tube – he knew the distinction well.)

This, I think, is the reason there have been so few depictions of the Underground in visual narrative form. Orson Welles once said that the only two things which could not be filmed were sexual intercourse and prayer. I take him to mean that they were the two human activities whose significance was entirely internal: they were happening to the people who were experiencing them in a manner which could only be experienced, and not depicted. The Underground is like that – not exactly like that, because there are significant differences between travelling on it and either having sex or praying, but it is on the same continuum, because its significance for us is internal. It's a going-in, a turning-in; not exactly a mystical state, but one which we know deep down inside ourselves is not an ordinary or routine condition. We escape it with distractions, or we try to switch off, but we can't entirely hide from it. That internal state, central to travel on the Underground, is something which it's very hard, perhaps impossible, to put on TV. Kim Stanley Robinson, in his SF novel *Forty Signs of Rain*, has a character float a theory about why this business of being underground connects so deeply with something inside us.

'He descended the Metro escalator into the ground. A weird action for a hominid to take – a religious experience. Following the shaman into the cave. We've never lost any of that.' And that, perhaps, is why people go quiet in the Underground. It's the only time we experience a combination of twenty-first-century technology (the trains), nineteenth-century technology and vision (the tunnels, the network) and our paleolithic deep self. A person on the Underground is experiencing the rare chance to be a twenty-first-century Victorian caveman. She is doing something we don't value enough, in the contemporary world: she is travelling in a direction we don't prize. She is going down and in. Down under the ground, and down into the self: into the city, into the world, into the streets and also into herself. That, finally, is what the Tube does most and does best. It takes us down and in.

# PENGUIN LINES

Choose Your Journey

## If you're looking for...

### Romantic Encounters

*Heads and Straights*
by Lucy Wadham
(the Circle line)

*Waterloo–City, City–Waterloo*
by Leanne Shapton
(the Waterloo & City line)

### Tales of Growing Up and Moving On

*Heads and Straights*
by Lucy Wadham
(the Circle line)

*A Good Parcel of English Soil*
by Richard Mabey
(the Metropolitan line)

*Mind the Child*
by Camila Batmanghelidjh and
Kids Company
(the Victoria line)

*The 32 Stops*
by Danny Dorling
(the Central line)

*A History of Capitalism*
*According to the Jubilee Line*
by John O'Farrell
(the Jubilee line)

*A Northern Line Minute*
by William Leith
(the Northern line)

**Laughter and Tears**

*Mind the Child*
by Camila Batmanghelidjh and
Kids Company
(the Victoria line)

*Heads and Straights*
by Lucy Wadham
(the Circle line)

**Breaking Boundaries**

*Drift*
by Philippe Parreno
(the Hammersmith & City line)

*Buttoned-Up*
by Fantastic Man
(the East London line)

*Waterloo–City, City–Waterloo*
by Leanne Shapton
(the Waterloo & City line)

*Earthbound*
by Paul Morley
(the Bakerloo line)

*Mind the Child*
by Camila Batmanghelidjh
and Kids Company
(the Victoria line)

*The Blue Riband*
by Peter York
(the Piccadilly line)

**A Bit of
Politics**

*The 32 Stops*
by Danny Dorling
(the Central line)

*A History of Capitalism
According to the Jubilee Line*
by John O'Farrell
(the Jubilee line)

**Musical
Direction**

*Heads and Straights*
by Lucy Wadham
(the Circle line)

*Earthbound*
by Paul Morley
(the Bakerloo line)

*The Blue Riband*
by Peter York
(the Piccadilly line)

**Tube Knowledge**

*What We Talk About When We Talk About The Tube*
by John Lanchester
(the District line)

*A Good Parcel of English Soil*
by Richard Mabey
(the Metropolitan line)

**A Breath of Fresh Air**

*A Good Parcel of English Soil*
by Richard Mabey
(the Metropolitan line)

**Design for Life**

*Waterloo–City, City–Waterloo*
by Leanne Shapton
(the Waterloo & City line)

*Buttoned-Up*
by Fantastic Man
(the East London line)

*Drift*
by Philippe Parreno
(the Hammersmith & City line)